SandCastle 3

Homonyms

The Top Is on Top

Kelly Doudna

ABDO Publishing Company

Published by SandCastle™, an imprint of ABDO Publishing Company, 4940 Viking Drive, Edina, Minnesota 55435.

Printed in the United States.

Photo credits: Brand X Pictures, Corbis Images, Comstock, Digital Vision, Eyewire Images, PhotoDisc

Library of Congress Cataloging-in-Publication Data

Doudna, Kelly, 1963-
      The top is on top / Kelly Doudna.
         p. cm. -- (Homonyms)
      Includes index.
      Summary: Photographs and simple text introduce homonyms, words that are spelled and sound the same but have different meanings.
         ISBN 1-57765-792-6
         1. English language--Homonyms--Juvenile literature. [1. English language--Homonyms.] I. Title.

PE1595 .D78 2002
428.1--dc21

2001053319

The SandCastle concept, content, and reading method have been reviewed and approved by a national advisory board including literacy specialists, librarians, elementary school teachers, early childhood education professionals, and parents.

Let Us Know

After reading the book, SandCastle would like you to tell us your stories about reading. What is your favorite page? Was there something hard that you needed help with? Share the ups and downs of learning to read. We want to hear from you! To get posted on the Abdo Publishing Company Web site, send us email at:

sandcastle@abdopub.com

About SandCastle™

Nonfiction books for the beginning reader

- Basic concepts of phonics are incorporated with integrated language methods of reading instruction. Most words are short, and phrases, letter sounds, and word sounds are repeated.

- Book levels are based on the ATOS™ for Books formula. Other considerations for readability include the number of words in each sentence, the number of characters in each word, and word lists based on curriculum frameworks.

- Full-color photography reinforces word meanings and concepts.

- "Words I Can Read" list at the end of each book teaches basic elements of grammar, helps the reader recognize the words in the text, and builds vocabulary.

- Reading levels are indicated by the number of flags on the castle.

SandCastle uses the following definitions for this series:

- Homographs: words that are spelled the same but sound different and have different meanings. *Easy memory tip: "-graph"= same look*

- Homonyms: words that are spelled and sound the same but have different meanings. *Easy memory tip: "-nym"= same name*

- Homophones: words that sound alike but are spelled differently and have different meanings. *Easy memory tip: "-phone"= sound alike*

Look for more SandCastle books in these three reading levels:

Level 1 (one flag)	**Level 2** (two flags)	**Level 3** (three flags)

Grades Pre-K to K 5 or fewer words per page	**Grades K to 1** 5 to 10 words per page	**Grades 1 to 2** 10 to 15 words per page

train   train

Homonyms are words that are spelled and sound the same but have different meanings.

I like to fish.

I use different kinds of tackle to catch them.

My brother plays football.

He tries to tackle the boy with the ball.

Dad and I play a game of tag.

We have fun together.

This shirt is for sale.

The price tag tells how much it costs.

Woodpeckers eat bugs.

They tap on tree trunks to find them.

My hands need washing.

I turn on the tap to let the water flow.

Lemonade tastes good on a hot summer day.

It has a tart flavor.

I enjoy dessert.

A small pie is called a tart.

The woman puts the money in the till.

It goes in the cash register.

Dad wants to plant a garden.

He must till the soil first.

I like to play baseball.

Dad gives me **tips** on how to play better.

This is my dog Spot.

The tips of his toes are white.

These cars must pay a **toll** to drive on this road.

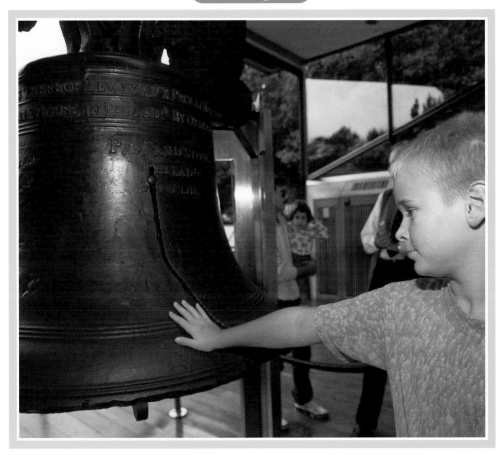

This bell used to **toll** loudly.

Now it hangs in a museum.

We are camping.

I like to **toast** marshmallows in the campfire.

What do I like to eat in the morning for breakfast?

(toast)

Words I Can Read

Nouns

A noun is a person, place, or thing

ball (BAWL) p. 7
baseball (BAYSS-bawl) p. 16
bell (BEL) p. 19
boy (BOI) p. 7
breakfast (BREK-fuhst) p. 21
brother (BRUHTH-ur) p. 7
bugs (BUHGZ) p. 10
campfire (KAMP-fire) p. 20
cars (KARZ) p. 18
cash register (KASH REJ-uh-stur) p. 14
day (DAY) p. 12
dessert (di-ZURT) p. 13
dog (DAWG) p. 17
flavor (FLAY-vur) p. 12
football (FUT-bal) p. 7
fun (FUHN) p. 8
game (GAYM) p. 8

garden (GARD-uhn) p. 15
hands (HANDZ) p. 11
homonyms (HOM-uh-nimz) p. 5
kinds (KINDEZ) p. 6
lemonade (lem-uh-NADE) p. 12
marshmallows (MARSH-mal-lohz) p. 20
meanings (MEE-ningz) p. 5
money (MUHN-ee) p. 14
morning (MOR-ning) p. 21
much (MUHCH) p. 9
museum (myoo-ZEE-uhm) p. 19
pie (PYE) p. 13
price tag (PREYESS TAG) p. 9
road (ROHD) p. 18

sale (SAYL) p. 9
shirt (SHURT) p. 9
soil (SOYL) p. 15
tackle (TAK-uhl) p. 6
tag (TAG) p. 8
tap (TAP) p. 11
tart (TART) p. 13
till (TIL) p. 14
tips (TIPSS) pp. 16, 17
toast (TOHST) p. 21
toes (TOHZ) p. 17
toll (TOHL) p. 18
train (TRANE) p. 4
tree trunks (TREE TRUHNGKSS) p. 10
water (WAW-tur) p. 11
woman (WUM-uhn) p. 14
woodpeckers (WUD-pek-urz) p. 10
words (WURDZ) p. 5

Proper Nouns

A proper noun is the name of a person, place, or thing

Dad (DAD) pp. 8, 15, 16   Spot (SPOT) p. 17

22

Pronouns

A pronoun is a word that replaces a noun

he (HEE) pp. 7, 15

I (EYE) pp. 6, 8, 11, 13, 16, 20, 21

it (IT) pp. 9, 12, 14, 19

me (MEE) p. 16

that (THAT) p. 5

them (THEM) pp. 6, 10

they (THAY) p. 10

this (THISS) p. 17

we (WEE) pp. 8, 20

what (WUHT) p. 21

Verbs

A verb is an action or being word

are (AR) pp. 5, 17, 20

called (KAWLD) p. 13

camping (KAMP-ing) p. 20

catch (KACH) p. 6

costs (KOSTSS) p. 9

do (DOO) p. 21

drive (DRIVE) p. 18

eat (EET) pp. 10, 21

enjoy (en-JOI) p. 13

find (FINDE) p. 10

fish (FISH) p. 6

flow (FLOH) p. 11

gives (GIVZ) p. 16

goes (GOHZ) p. 14

hangs (HANGZ) p. 19

has (HAZ) p. 12

have (HAV) pp. 5, 8

is (IZ) pp. 9, 13, 17

let (LET) p. 11

like (LIKE) pp. 6, 16, 20, 21

must (MUHST) pp. 15, 18

need (NEED) p. 11

pay (PAY) p. 18

plant (PLANT) p. 15

play (PLAY) pp. 8, 16

plays (PLAYZ) p. 7

puts (PUTSS) p. 14

sound (SOUND) p. 5

spelled (SPELD) p. 5

tackle (TAK-uhl) p. 7

tap (TAP) p. 10

tastes (TAYSTSS) p. 12

tells (TELZ) p. 9

till (TIL) p. 15

toast (TOHST) p. 20

toll (TOHL) p. 19

train (TRANE) p. 4

tries (TRIZE) p. 7

turn (TURN) p. 11

use (YOOZ) p. 6

used (YOOZD) p. 19

wants (WONTSS) p. 15

washing (WOSH-ing) p. 11

Adjectives

An adjective describes something

different (DIF-ur-uhnt)
pp. 5, 6

good (gud) p. 12

his (HIZ) p. 17

hot (HOT) p. 12

my (MYE) pp. 7, 11, 17

same (SAYM) p. 5

small (SMAWL) p. 13

summer (SUHM-ur)
p. 12

tart (TART) p. 12

these (THEEZ) p. 18

this (THISS)
pp. 9, 18, 19

white (WITE) p. 17

Adverbs

An adverb tells how, when, or where something happens

better (BET-ur) p. 16

first (FURST) p. 15

how (HOU) p. 9

loudly (LOUD-lee) p. 19

now (NOU) p. 19

together
(tuh-GETH-ur) p. 8